BILINGÜE/BILINGUAL

Hacer gráficas/
Making Graphs

Pictografías
Pictographs

por/by Vijaya Khisty Bodach

CAPSTONE PRESS
a capstone imprint

A+ Books are published by Capstone Press,
1710 Roe Crest Drive, North Mankato, Minnesota 56003.
www.capstonepub.com

Books published by Capstone Press are manufactured with paper
containing at least 10 percent post-consumer waste.

Library of Congress Cataloging-in-Publication Data
Bodach, Vijaya.
 [Pictographs. Spanish & English]
 Pictografías / por Vijay Khisty Bodach = Pictographs / by Vijaya Khisty Bodach.
   p. cm.—(A+ bilingüe. Hacer gráficas = Bilingual. Making graphs)
 Includes index.
 Summary: "Uses simple text and photographs to describe how to make and use pictographs—in
both English and Spanish"—Provided by publisher.
  ISBN 978-1-4296-6101-0 (library binding)   ISBN 978-1-4296-8544-3 (softcover)
 1. Mathematics—Charts, diagrams, etc.—Juvenile literature. 2. Graphic methods—Study and
teaching (Elementary)—Juvenile literature. 3. Mathematical statistics—Study and teaching
(Elementary)—Juvenile literature. 4. Signs and symbols—Juvenile literature. 5. Games in
mathematics education—Juvenile literature. I. Title. II. Title: Pictographs.
 QA90.B6218 2011
 001.4'226—dc22   2010042251

Credits

Heather Adamson, editor; Strictly Spanish, translation services; Juliette Peters, designer;
   Eric Manske, bilingual book designer; Wanda Winch, media researcher; Kelly Garvin,
   photo stylist; Sarah Bennett, production specialist

Photo Credits

All photos Capstone Press/Karon Dubke except page 10 (bottom) Getty Images Inc./Stone/
   Daniel Bolser, page 11 Brand X, and page 18 iStockphoto/Andresr.

Note to Parents, Teachers, and Librarians

Hacer gráficas/Making Graphs uses color photographs and a nonfiction format to introduce
readers to graphing concepts in both English and Spanish. *Pictografías/Pictographs* is designed
to be read aloud to a pre-reader, or to be read independently by an early reader. Images and
activities encourage mathematical thinking in early readers and listeners. The book encourages
further learning by including the following sections: Table of Contents, Glossary, Internet Sites,
and Index. Early readers may need assistance using these features.

Printed in the United States of America in North Mankato, Minnesota.
102011   006405CGS12

Table of Contents

Tabla de contenidos

Look at all these bunnies!
Do we have more bunnies that are
white or spotted brown?

¡Mira todos esos conejitos!
¿Tenemos más conejitos blancos o
con manchas marrones?

Let's put the animals in rows.
Then we can compare.

Vamos a poner a los animales en filas.
Luego nosotros podemos comparar.

The row of white bunnies is longer.
We have more white bunnies
than spotted bunnies.

La fila de conejitos blancos es más larga.
Nosotros tenemos más conejitos blancos
que conejitos con manchas marrones.

Using pictures is easier than using animals.
Pictographs use pictures to show how many.

Usar dibujos es más fácil que usar animales.
Las pictografías usan dibujos para mostrar
qué cantidad hay.

This pictograph shows yellow flowers are most popular in this bunch. There are the fewest white flowers.

1 picture = 1 flower/1 dibujo = 1 flor

Esta pictografía muestra que las flores amarillas son las más populares en este ramo. Hay menos flores blancas.

We are getting ready for a big party. Let's make a pictograph of the party supplies.

Nos preparamos para una fiesta grande. Vamos a hacer una pictografía de los artículos para la fiesta.

Each picture stands for five items.
We need lots of balloons but only
a few candles.

Party Supplies/
Artículos para la fiesta

balloons/
globos

plates/
platos

napkins/
servilletas

candles/
velitas

1 picture = 5 / 1 dibujo = 5

Cada dibujo representa cinco artículos.
Nosotros necesitamos muchos globos
pero sólo unas pocas velitas.

Milk, juice, or soda pop?
Which party drink will kids choose?

¿Leche, jugo o gaseosa?
¿Qué bebida elegirán los niños en la fiesta?

Juice was the most popular choice.
Fewer kids drank soda or milk.

favorite drink / bebida favorita

1 picture = 2 drinks
1/2 picture = 1 drink
/
1 dibujo = 2 bebidas
1/2 dibujo = 1 bebida

El jugo fue la elección más popular.
Menos niños bebieron gaseosa o leche.